The Only I AM

Anchored in the Unchanging God

Bonnie Jean Schaefer

Dream Doers Publishing LLC

Published by Dream Doers Publishing LLC
Tobaccoville, North Carolina

Unless otherwise noted, all Scripture quotations are taken from the Christian Standard Bible®, Copyright © 2017 by Holman Bible Publishers. Used by permission. Christian Standard Bible® and CSB® are federally registered trademarks of Holman Bible Publishers.

Pronouns referring to God have been capitalized for emphasis.

Book Cover by Bonnie Jean Schaefer

Paperback ISBN: 978-0-9907463-7-9

CONTENTS

Why This Book Exists   1

Opening Prayer   5

1. The Great I AM   7

2. The Eternal I AM   12

3. The Triune I AM   18

4. The Holy I AM   24

5. The Unique I AM   31

6. The Active I AM   43

7. The Transforming I AM   53

Acknowledgements   62

About the Author   63

Why This Series Exists   65

The League of Adventurous Authors   68

WHY THIS BOOK EXISTS

I thought I knew God.

Having accepted Christ as my Savior at age four, I've never known life without God. For over four decades, I've been seeking Him and walking with Him and talking with Him. I studied Bible in college at Cedarville, choosing theology over professional writing because I wanted to prepare for life, not just a career.

Earning that Bible degree strengthened my faith foundation and allows me to filter the experiences of life through the truth of God's word.

But I still approached personal growth the way most people do — starting with me. Who am I? What do I want? Why? What are my goals? How do I assess my life and make improvements? I consumed books and courses and programs that all began with self-evaluation and self-determination. I dared not go all in on embracing what I was learning, however, because I recognized God was missing from those "self-help" materials. So I've spent decades trying to figure out how to align the truth of God's word with personal transformation.

About seven years ago, I realized personal development doesn't start with me. It starts with God. So I spent prayerful time and effort detailing my core convictions about who God is in relation to me: my Creator, King, Savior, Father, Friend, Helper, and Judge.

This revelation changed my entire perspective. If God is truly the anchor and core of my existence — especially in a world where everything seems to be accelerating and shifting at breakneck speed — then shouldn't I understand the God who doesn't change before I try to change anything about myself?

At first, I focused on anchoring myself in the truth of God's Word. But then I discovered there's an even more foundational step: anchoring myself in who God is at His very essence, before studying what He says or does. This realization deepened as I struggled with prayer. I knew I should honor God for who He is before asking for what I want, but I kept wanting to jump straight into my dreams, goals, petitions, problems, and struggles without truly recognizing who I was praying to.

That's when I began what I call "pray-thinking" — contemplating God's nature in conversation with Him. This approach felt natural because for decades, I've been a writer who processes thoughts through words, especially in my daily journaling. Instead of just recording my day, I pray through writing each night because when I have to find words to write, I communicate more clearly and think more deeply.

So I expanded this style of prayer-writing to focus entirely on God and His essence rather than on me and my concerns. Drawing from everything I'd learned since childhood, my Bible education, and over four decades of Christian life, I compiled my thoughts about who God really is at His core.

But I didn't want to teach about God. I wanted to talk to God about who He is and let you as a reader listen in on the conversation so that you can deepen your own prayer life as you seek to know God.

This isn't meant to be an academic theology text. It's a conversation with God. Through conversations like this is how I dig into truth and grow. The subject just happens to be God Himself.

This book is intentionally short. It's designed to help you grasp the big picture of who God is without being overwhelmed by mountains of pages. My hope is that the words and concepts will spark your own ideas, prayers, and studies of your own.

My prayer is that as you read, you'll discover what I'm still discovering: knowing God is the foundation of life.

Each chapter is written as a prayer, a genuine conversation with God about different aspects of His character. In other words, you're overhearing someone wrestling with, wondering about, and worshipping the God who reveals Himself as "I AM."

This format is intentional. I believe we learn about God best not through detached study, but through engaged relationship. When we approach God's nature with both our minds and our hearts, transformation happens naturally.

Read it slowly. This isn't meant to be consumed quickly. Each chapter explores profound truths about God's nature that deserve time to settle into your heart and mind.

Read it prayerfully. Let the words become your words. Let the questions become your questions. Let the worship become your worship. Let it spark ideas on how you can expand the prayer in your own words.

Read it personally. While the book uses "I" throughout, substitute your own name and story. Make this conversation between you and God about who He is and what that means for your life.

Read it repeatedly. These truths about God are inexhaustible. Come back to chapters that particularly impact you. Let them marinate in your soul over time.

But reading it does you no good if you don't integrate these truths into your life. So I challenge you to:

- **Apply it practically.** Each chapter includes implications for how knowing God should change how you live. Don't let these remain theoretical. Put them into practice.

- **Let it shape your prayers.** Use what you learn about God to deepen your prayer life. When you know who you're talking to, it changes how you talk to Him.

- **Share it with others.** God's nature is meant to be proclaimed. Talk about what you're learning with fellow believers. Let your growing knowledge of God encourage others in their own journey.

God desires to be known. He has revealed Himself to invite us into the wonder of walking with Him.

So come with an open heart. Come with honest questions. Come ready to be changed.

Because when you truly encounter the Great I AM — self-existent, eternal, triune, holy, personal, and speaking — you will inevitably be transformed.

And that transformation is exactly what He intends.

Let the conversation begin.

OPENING PRAYER

HEAVENLY FATHER,

You are the great I AM — self-existent, eternal, and un-changing.

You have no beginning and no end. Before the foundations of the world, You were. Throughout time, You are. When time ends, You always will be.

You are holy, sovereign, and infinitely beyond my compre-hension, yet You have made Yourself known to me through Your Word, through Christ, and through Your Spirit.

Lord, I long to know You not just for what You do for me but for who You are. Open my mind to grasp Your self-existence and understand the implications of the fact You need nothing and no one to sustain You.

Teach me to marvel at Your eternal nature. Help me to rest in the truth that You are always faithful, always just, always loving, always holy, and just...always.

You are Father, Son, and Holy Spirit. One God in three Persons, coequal and united. Though my mind cannot fully com-prehend this mystery, help my heart to trust in the truth of Your Word. Reveal to me how each Person of the Trinity has been at work in my life, drawing me into fellowship with You.

God, increase my awe of Your holiness. Let me see Your majesty, that I may live in reverence and worship. Increase my faith in Your sovereignty so that I may rest in the knowledge that nothing is outside of Your control. Increase my understanding of Your justice so that I may walk in righteousness. Increase my experience of Your mercy and grace so that I may live in gratitude and extend that grace to others.

Lord, I do not want just knowledge about You. I want to know You and experience life with You. I want to love You with all my heart, soul, mind, and strength. So show me more of who You are as I seek You daily in Your Word, meditate on Your truth, and hunger for more of You. Give me the wisdom to discern what is true, the humility to accept what I do not yet understand, and the faith to trust in Your perfect character.

Remove any distractions or idols that compete for my attention. Silence the doubts and lies that distort my understanding of You. Fill me with the Holy Spirit, that I may be led into all truth and grow in deeper intimacy with You.

Father, I pray as Moses did: "Show me Your glory." I want to see You, to know You, to be transformed by Your presence. May my life reflect Your truth and be a testimony of Your greatness.

Thank You, Lord, for revealing Yourself to me. Keep me in Your truth, ground me in Your Word, and let my life glorify You forever.

In Christ,
Amen.

1

—·—

THE GREAT I AM

UNDERSTANDING GOD'S SELF-EXISTENCE

FATHER,

You amaze me. You are so different from anyone and everything I know. Like the fact that You have no beginning. No cause. No origin story.

You are self-existent, meaning You exist by Your own nature without being caused, created, or sustained by anything else. You require nothing outside of Yourself to exist.

How is that possible?!?

Everything I know has a beginning and depends on something else. Every person I meet was born from parents. Every tree sprouted from a seed that came from another tree. Every breath I take depends on oxygen.

But You...

You simply are. You need nothing. You depend on nothing. You are sustained by nothing outside Yourself.

You are the Great I AM.

I AM WHO I AM

When Moses stood before the burning bush, trembling and uncertain, he asked You for a name. Something to call You. Something to explain who You are.

And You answered:

"I AM WHO I AM. This is what you are to say to the Israelites: I AM has sent me to you" (Exodus 3:14).

You didn't say, "I was created by..." You didn't say, "I depend on..." You said, "I AM."

That never made much sense to me. I want to understand now. Why "I AM?"

Why not God, the awesome and mighty Creator of the world and King of the Universe?

Why I AM?

What is significant and marvelous about I AM? What does it mean?

Self-existent. Independent. Uncaused.

No one created You. No force sustains You. No source feeds You. No power supports You.

Everything else in existence depends on something. A plant needs soil, sunlight, and rain. A river needs a source. A child needs parents. A fire needs oxygen. A thought needs a mind. A song needs a singer.

But You...

You need nothing.

You are self-existent, uncreated, uncaused, completely independent.

You Are Not Like Me

Lord, my mind wrestles with this.

Everything in my experience is dependent. I depend on air to breathe, food to energize, sleep to function. I depend on my parents for my existence, my body for my life, my heart for every beat.

Even my thoughts depend on my brain. My emotions depend on my thoughts. My strength depends on rest.

I am a creature of need. I require. I depend. I lack.

But You are not like me.

You do not need anything to exist. You are perfectly complete in Yourself. How is it that You do not lack anything?

What does it mean that You simply ARE?

Your Self-Existence Means...

As the self-existent I AM, You are completely independent. You do not need anyone or anything to exist. You are You forever and always no matter what.

You don't need me, yet You created me anyway. You love me anyway. You want a relationship with me anyway. This isn't because You're lonely or lacking. You are perfectly complete in Yourself. You created me because You chose to share Your love, not because You needed to receive mine.

You are the source of all existence. Including mine. Everything that is comes from You. Everything I am comes from You. You are the uncaused Cause, the original Source, the Creator of all things. Without You, nothing would exist. With You, everything finds its beginning.

You are the unchanging foundation. You don't improve or decline. You don't get stronger or weaker. You don't learn or forget. You are the Rock that never shifts, the Truth that never wavers, the God whose nature never changes.

Your love for me is uncaused. You don't love me because I'm lovable or because You need my love in return. You love me because You are love — pure, overflowing, and completely independent. Your love doesn't depend on my performance, my faithfulness, or my response. It flows from who You are, not from what I do.

Too often, my pride wants to reverse this. I want to be independent, to need nothing and no one, to be self-sufficient. But even in my rebellious moments of trying to live without You, I'm still completely dependent on You for my very existence.

I cannot exist apart from You, but You exist perfectly without me.

And yet You choose me anyway.

I Bow Before You

I cannot grasp You fully, but I can bow before You.

I cannot contain You in my understanding, but I can trust You.

I cannot reduce You to human logic, but I can rejoice that You want me.

Father, let me never treat You like a mere concept to be studied or a force to be analyzed.

You are not a theory. You are not an idea. You are not a distant deity confined to books and doctrine.

You are the living God.

You are **the Great I AM.**

You, who need nothing, choose to reveal Yourself to me.

You, who lack nothing, chose to create me.

You, who are completely independent, choose to love me.

You are self-sufficient and complete in Yourself, and You invite me in. You call me Yours.

Oh what peace that brings to my aching, needy soul! I stand in awe of You, the only truly independent Being, and I cling to You, the source of my existence.

You are I AM, and I am because You are.

In Christ,

Amen.

2

THE ETERNAL I AM

BEFORE TIME BEGAN

FATHER,

I exist in time.

I measure my life in days and years. I count the hours. Map the minutes. Feel the seconds of time constantly ticking forward.

But You do not move through time. Time moves through You. Because You are eternal.

Eternal means existing without beginning or end, completely outside the bounds of time.

You do not wait for the future. You hold it in Your hands.

You do not dwell in the past. You see it as clearly as this present moment.

Before anything existed — the first sunrise, the first heartbeat, the first breath of creation — You were.

And even when the world as I know it comes to an end, You will still be.

You are from everlasting to everlasting.

Before the Beginning Began

"Before the mountains were born, before You gave birth to the earth and the world, from eternity to eternity, You are God" (Psalm 90:2).

You have no beginning in time. No moment marks Your first existence.

But when I try to imagine the time before time, my mind struggles.

It's hard to imagine a "time" before time when only You existed. That sounds lonely to me, but You are perfectly complete in Yourself — Father, Son, and Holy Spirit in eternal fellowship.

There was no "before" for You, because "before" requires time, and time did not exist.

You are eternal, existing outside of past, present, and future.

And yet...

You created time.

The Creator of Time

Time did not create You. You created time. With only words!

"In the beginning God created the heavens and the earth" (Genesis 1:1).

That was the first moment.

Not just the first moment of the universe, but the first moment of time itself.

Before that, there were no ticking clocks. No passing seconds. No yesterday. No tomorrow. Only the eternal now in which You dwell.

Time was not an accident. It was not a force outside of You, shaping You.

It was something You spoke into existence, a framework for creation, a river through which life would flow.

This means that You are the Lord of time. You created it, and You rule over it. It does not control You; You control it.

You are unbound by time. You do not age. You do not change. You do not grow weary. You are not subject to decay or loss.

You are sovereign over time. You see the end from the beginning. You are never surprised, never late, never early.

I Am Trapped in Time – But You Are Not

Lord, my life is marked by time. I track what time I go to bed and what time I wake up.

Time determines when I show up for work, eat my meals, play with my family, and plan the future.

I live moment by moment, second by second, always moving forward. I remember the past but can't return to it. I wonder about the future but can't skip ahead to it.

But You are outside of all of it. You do not experience time as a sequence of events. Because although I experience life like reading a book one page at a time, You see the entire story at once.

To You, my birth and my last breath are equally present. To You, the first day of creation and the last day of this world are equally before You.

You do not see time the way I do.

When You say, "I am the Alpha and the Omega, the first and the last, the beginning and the end" (Revelation 22:13), You are declaring that all of time is held within You.

You made time for me. Although You don't live within its constraints, in Your infinite wisdom You determined that I needed the structure of time.

Living in Time Under the Eternal God

Since You are outside of time and hold all of history in Your hands, why do I worry about tomorrow?

Why do I fear the unknown when it is not unknown to You?

Why do I regret the past when You stand outside of it and can redeem it?

Why do I rush through life when You are never in a hurry?

I am impatient, restless, eager to see results immediately. But You are never rushed. You work according to Your perfect timing. One day to You is as a thousand years and a thousand years as one day. That frustrates me when I want what I want NOW but am stuck in limbo waiting for what I've requested.

So I want to live an unhurried life. I want to cultivate patience rather than zip through life. I want to learn to redeem the time You've given me.

I look at my past and see wasted years. Missed opportunities. Failures. Regrets. But nothing surprised You. You saw every moment before it happened, and You have a plan and purpose that spans beyond my understanding of time.

Help me trust in You and Your timing.

Your Eternal Perspective

Because You are eternal, You see my entire life — past, present, and future — all at once.

You know how my current struggles will strengthen me for future challenges I can't yet see.

You know how my past failures will become testimonies of Your grace in ways I can't imagine.

You know how my present prayers will be answered in Your perfect timing according to what is best for me.

When I can't see the bigger picture, You can. When I'm lost in the details of today, You see the grand design that spans eternity.

When I feel like time is running out, You remind me that You are outside of time altogether.

When I feel forgotten in the waiting, You show me that Your timing is always perfect.

Safe In Your Eternal Arms

Before Your eternity, I can only surrender by releasing my need to control time.

I lay down my fear of the future and rest in the One who is outside of time yet walks with me in it.

Father, I will trust You when time seems to move too slowly, when prayers seem unanswered, when life feels like it's slipping away. When the future is uncertain.

You are **the Eternal I AM**.

You are not limited by time. You are not bound by the past. You are not worried about the future.

And because You are eternal, I have eternal security. I am held by the One who was, who is, and who is to come.

You created time, but You also created eternity in my heart. One day, I will step out of time and into Your eternal presence, where there are no more clocks, no more deadlines, no more waiting.

Until then, I will live in time, but I will live under the peace of knowing You are eternal.

And in You, I am safe.

In Christ,

Amen.

3

THE TRIUNE I AM

THE MYSTERY OF THE TRINITY

FATHER,

You are **the Great I AM** — self-existent, uncaused, independent of all things.

You are **the Eternal One** — beyond time, unbound by past or future.

But now I stand at the threshold of a mystery that stretches my mind to its breaking point:

You are not just one. You are three in one.

Trinity means one God existing simultaneously as three distinct Persons — Father, Son, and Holy Spirit. Each fully God, yet not three Gods. One God.

This makes no sense to me. How can one equal three? How can three equal one?

Everything in my experience screams that this is impossible. One person is one person. Three people are three people.

But You are not bound by my experience or my logic.

You are God, and You have revealed this about Yourself.

"Let Us Make Man in Our Image"

From the very beginning, You deliberately disclosed the first clue about Your triune nature when You used Elohim, a plural form of God, paired with bara, the singular word for created:

"In the beginning God created the heavens and the earth" (Genesis 1:1).

It's no accident that the Bible opens with a name that signals both singularity and abundance! And later in that same chapter, we get clue number two:

"Then God said, 'Let Us make man in Our image, according to Our likeness'" (Genesis 1:26a).

Wait. Stop right there.

"Let **Us**?" "**Our** image?"

Who were You talking to, Lord? You're the only God. There is no other.

Yet You said "Us." You said "Our."

Who were You speaking to? Not the angels. They didn't create anything. You did.

You were speaking within Yourself. Father to Son. Son to Spirit. Spirit with Father.

One God in perfect internal communion.

But how? How does that work?

The Mystery Unfolds

Throughout Scripture, You don't give me a systematic theology textbook explanation. You don't hand me a neat diagram.

Instead, You scatter clues like breadcrumbs, inviting me to follow the trail of truth.

The Father is God. You planned redemption. You sent the Son. You are the source. "Yet for us there is one God, the Father. All things are from Him, and we exist for Him" (1 Corinthians 8:6a).

The Son is God. Jesus claimed equality with You. He accepted worship. He forgave sins, and this is something only God can do. "In the beginning was the Word, and the Word was with God, and the Word was God" (John 1:1).

The Spirit is God. Not a force. Not an influence. A Person who can be grieved, who speaks, who decides. Who knows the heart, exercises moral authority, and judges sin with immediate divine consequences as demonstrated in Acts. "'Annanias,' Peter asked, 'why has Satan filled your heart to lie to the Holy Spirit and keep back part of the proceeds of the land? Wasn't it yours while you possessed it? And after it was sold, wasn't it at your disposal? Why is it that you planned this thing in your heart? You have not lied to people but to God" (Acts 5:3-4).

Three Persons. Each called God. Each with divine attributes. Each doing divine works.

Yet You insist there is only one God.

My brain wants to choose: either three gods or one Person playing three roles.

But You refuse both options. You are three **and** one. Simultaneously. Mysteriously.

The Trinity in Redemption

I see Your three-in-oneness most clearly in my salvation.

The Father willed my rescue. You planned the method of salvation before the foundation of the world — one perfect sacrifice to cover all the sins of all humanity throughout all time.

The Son accomplished my rescue. Jesus lived as fully man and fully God, died having done nothing wrong, and rose again to defeat death, the ultimate curse of sin.

The Spirit applies my rescue. The Spirit convinced me, convicted me, and sealed me.

But I had to choose You. Because You give every person a choice: believe on the Lord Jesus Christ and be saved, or reject Him and experience eternal death.

I chose to believe.

My salvation isn't a result of three gods working separately but from one God working in perfect unity through three Persons.

The Father didn't send Himself to die — He sent the Son. The Son laid down His life and took it up again — not alone but by the Father's will and the Spirit's power. The Spirit doesn't point to Himself — He points to the Son and glorifies the Father.

Each Person distinct. Each role unique. Yet perfectly unified in purpose and love.

Why the Trinity Matter?

You were never lonely. Before creation, perfect love already existed between Father, Son, and Spirit. You didn't create me because You needed relationship. You created me to share the relationship You already perfectly possess.

Love is not just what You do; it's who You are. Love requires relationship, and relationship exists eternally within Your triune nature. "God is love" (1 John 4:8) isn't just a nice saying. It's the fundamental reality of Your being.

When I feel isolated, misunderstood, or fractured by conflict, I remember that You don't theorize about relationship. You **are** relationship. The Father has never known a moment without the

Son. The Son has never spoken a word the Spirit didn't carry. You are the blueprint for connection, the living definition of unity in diversity. I don't have to wonder if true relationship is possible. I just look at You.

And You invited me **into it**. Jesus prayed, "I have given them the glory You have given Me, so that they may be one, even as We are one" (John 17:22). You're not inviting me into some abstract spiritual experience. You're pulling me into the same love, the same unity, the same eternal bond that defines Your existence. My relationship with you isn't a shadow of the real thing. It's a share in it.

The Limits of My Understanding

I cannot solve You like a math problem. I cannot dissect You like a science experiment.

You are infinite, and I am finite. You are Creator, and I am creation.

The fact that I cannot fully comprehend the Trinity doesn't make it untrue. It makes You God.

If I could understand everything about You, You wouldn't be worth worshipping.

If You fit completely within my mind, You'd be too small to save me.

So I embrace the mystery. I bow before what I cannot grasp. I worship what I cannot contain.

Mystery, Yet Mine

Father, You created me and call me Your child.

Son, You redeemed me and call me Your friend.

Spirit, You dwell in me and call me Your temple.

I don't have to understand how You are three-in-one to know that You are. I don't have to solve the mystery to trust the God who reveals it. I don't have to comprehend Your infinite nature to rest in Your perfect love.

You are one God — Father, Son, and Holy Spirit.

You are beyond my understanding but not beyond my worship.

You are mystery, but You are also mine.

And that is enough.

In Christ,

Amen.

4

---·---

THE HOLY I AM

GOD'S ESSENTIAL NATURE

FATHER,

You have revealed Yourself to me:

- As the Great I AM, self-existent and independent of all things.

- As the Eternal One, unbound by time and sovereign over all history.

- As the Triune God, Father, Son, and Spirit in perfect unity.

But now I need to understand something deeper. Something that makes me uncomfortable. Something that separates me from You: holiness.

Holy means completely set apart, morally perfect, utterly pure and separate from all sin and corruption.

And that's exactly who You are.

This isn't just another nice quality You happen to possess. This is the core of Your being. The foundation of everything else about You.

You are holy. I am not.

Holy, Holy, Holy

Isaiah had a glimpse of Your holiness:

"In the year that King Uzziah died, I saw the Lord seated on a high and lofty throne, and the hem of His robe filled the temple. Seraphim were standing above Him; they each had six wings: with two they covered their faces, with two they covered their feet, and with two they flew. And one called to another: 'Holy, holy, holy is the Lord of Armies; His glory fills the whole earth" (Isaiah 6:1-3).

The angels don't cry, "Love, love, love," though You are perfect love.

They don't cry, "Power, power, power," though You are all-powerful.

They don't cry, "Mercy, mercy, mercy," though You are infinitely merciful.

They cry, **"Holy, holy, holy!"**

Why? What is it about Your holiness that makes even angels cover their faces?

Your holiness is the essence that defines every other attribute You possess.

Your love is holy love. Your power is holy power. Your mercy is holy mercy. Your justice is holy justice.

Everything about You is set apart, pure, perfect.

You are in a category all Your own.

A Vision That Humbles Me

Isaiah saw You, Lord. Actually saw You.

Angels covered their faces. Beings who live in Your presence couldn't even look at You directly.

The foundations of heaven shook at Your voice. Smoke filled the temple.

And Isaiah's response?

"Woe is me for I am ruined because I am a man of unclean lips and live among a people of unclean lips, and because my eyes have seen the King, the Lord of Armies" (Isaiah 6:5).

One glimpse of Your holiness, and he was distraught. Not inspired. Not encouraged. Not filled with warm feelings.

Undone. Terrified. Aware that he was about to die.

This is what happens when sinful humanity encounters absolute holiness.

What Does It Mean That You Are Holy?

Lord, I need to understand this better because everything in my culture tries to make You safe, approachable, manageable.

But Your holiness makes You none of those things.

You are completely separate from sin. Not just "better than sinners." Completely other. There is no corruption in You. No compromise. No shadow of moral failure.

"This is the message we have heard from Him and declare to you: God is light, and there is absolutely no darkness in Him" (1 John 1:5).

I can't even imagine what that's like. My thoughts are often tainted by selfishness. My motives are often mixed. My actions are often imperfect.

But You? Your thoughts are perfectly pure. Your motives are perfectly righteous. Your actions are perfectly just.

You are morally perfect. Not just "really good." Infinitely, unchangeably perfect. Your holiness sets the standard for what goodness even means.

"Your eyes are too pure to look on evil, and You cannot tolerate wrongdoing" (Habakkuk 1:13a).

This means sin is something You cannot coexist with, not simply something. Your very nature demands separation from anything unholy.

Where Does That Leave Me?

If You are this holy, then where do I stand?

I like to compare myself to others. It makes me feel better about myself.

"I'm not as bad as that person over there."

"At least I don't lie like they do."

"I try to be good most of the time."

But standing before You, comparison becomes meaningless. Next to Your holiness, my best efforts are "filthy rags" (Isaiah 64:6).

You are light; I am darkness.

You are pure; I am stained.

You are perfect; I am broken.

If I were to step into Your presence as I am, I would be destroyed. Not because You're mean, but because Your holiness demands the destruction of sin.

It's like trying to bring a pile of dead leaves into a consuming fire. The fire doesn't hate the leaves. It's just the nature of fire to consume anything combustible.

Your Holiness Means Judgment

Lord, this is where I want to look away. Because Your holiness is terrifying.

Since You are holy, You must judge sin. You cannot ignore it. You cannot excuse it. You cannot pretend it doesn't matter.

Sin must be punished, or *You would cease to be holy!*

This is why Adam and Eve were expelled from Eden. Why the flood came. Why Sodom and Gomorrah were destroyed. Why the Law required blood sacrifice.

Sin isn't just "making mistakes" or "nobody's perfect."

Sin is rebellion against Your holiness. It's cosmic treason against the perfectly pure Creator.

And the penalty is death:

"For the wages of sin is death" (Romans 6:23a).

I don't like this. It makes me uncomfortable. But it's true whether I like it or not.

The Impossible Solution

But something happened in Isaiah's vision that gives me hope.

As he trembled before You, a seraphim flew to him with a burning coal from the altar. It touched his lips, and the angel said:

"Then one of the seraphim flew to me, and in his hand was a glowing coal that he had taken from the altar with tongs. He touched my mouth with it and said, 'Now that this has touched your lips, your iniquity is removed and your sin is atoned for" (Isaiah 6:7).

Isaiah didn't cleanse himself. He couldn't.

You cleansed him.

The Holy One made a way for unholy sinners to stand in Your presence.

That altar in Isaiah's vision pointed to a greater altar, that of the Cross where Your holiness and Your love would meet in the most shocking way possible.

Jesus — perfectly holy, perfectly sinless — took my judgment upon Himself.

"He made the One who did not know sin to be sin for us, so that in Him we might become the righteousness of God" (2 Corinthians 5:21).

Your holiness didn't change. Your standards didn't lower. Your justice wasn't compromised.

Instead, You satisfied Your own holiness by taking my punishment on Yourself.

That's costly, holy love.

Clothed in Christ

How can someone like me stand before a holy God?

Only by Your grace. Only through Jesus' blood. Only because You made a way.

I don't belong in Your presence. I deserve to be consumed by Your holiness.

But because of Christ, I can stand before You clothed in His righteousness instead of my filthy rags.

So my response has to be:

Humility — I fall before You, fully aware that I have no right to be here.

Repentance — I turn from my sin because I finally see how offensive it is to Your holiness.

Worship — I bow before the God who is so holy that He cannot tolerate sin, yet so loving that He made a way for sinners.

Surrender — I give You my life because You alone are worthy of it.

Lord, I don't want to tame You in my mind. I don't want to make You safe and manageable.

You are holy. Terrifyingly, beautifully, perfectly holy.

And somehow, impossibly, You have made me holy, too. You didn't do so by changing Your standards but by covering me with Christ's perfection.

Let that reality transform how I live.

In Christ,

Amen.

5

—·—

THE UNIQUE I AM

THE CHARACTER AND PERSONALITY OF GOD

FATHER,

You are self-existent, eternal, triune, and holy.

But You're not just a collection of divine attributes floating in space.

You are a **Person**. A living, thinking, feeling, deciding God with a personality so vast and complete that I'll spend eternity discovering new depths of who You are.

Character refers to the essential qualities that define who You are. **Personality** is how those qualities express themselves in relationship.

And You have both in perfect fullness.

You could choose to remain distant, an impersonal force managing the universe from afar. But You don't. You reveal Yourself. You engage. You relate.

You are the living God who has a mind, will, emotions, and desires.

So who are You? What are You like when I really get to know You?

The Foundation of Your Character

Through Scripture, creation, and Christ, You show me who You are.

But I need to stop thinking about You the way I think about myself.

I have personality traits that shift with my mood. I have character qualities that I'm still developing. I can be patient one day and short-tempered the next.

You're not like that.

Your attributes aren't qualities You're working on or characteristics You balance. They are eternal realities of who You are. Perfect expressions of Your unchanging nature.

Every aspect of Your character is absolute. Unwavering. Complete.

So what have You revealed about Yourself?

You Are Omnipresent

You are always here. Fully here.

"Where can I go to escape Your Spirit? Where can I flee from Your presence? If I go up to heaven, You are there; if I make my bed in Sheol, You are there" (Psalm 139:7-8).

Not just keeping an eye on me from a distance. Not checking in occasionally when You remember I exist.

All of You is present with all of me all the time, everywhere I go.

I can't escape You, nor can I summon You...because You never leave.

This should feel suffocating, but it doesn't. It feels safe.

You're in the room when I pray, when I doubt, when I mess up, when I pretend everything's fine. You don't step out when things get messy. You don't walk away when I disappoint You.

You're not impressed by my performance, and You're not confused by my silence.

You're here. Waiting for me to stop trying to handle life on my own and start seeking You first.

But You're not just present; You're purposeful. You didn't create me to survive without You. You made me to walk with You, step by step, day by day.

You promised, "I will never leave you or abandon you" (Hebrews 13:5b). You're not background music in my life. You're the main conversation.

And because You're always present, You know me completely.

You Are Omniscient

You know everything. Not just the facts. Me.

"Lord, You have searched me and known me. You know when I sit down and when I stand up; You understand my thoughts from far away" (Psalm 139:1-2).

You know what I'm feeling before I find words for it. You see the dreams I'm afraid to admit and the fears I try to bury. You know the motives behind my actions, the insecurities I hide, the thoughts I'm ashamed of.

You understand my heart when I can't even understand it myself. You get what I'm going through when no one else does. You see through my pretending to what I really need.

And somehow, You still want to be with me.

This should terrify me, but it doesn't anymore. Because You don't use Your knowledge to shame me. You use it to lead me.

"Before a word is on my tongue, you know all about it, Lord" (Psalm 139:4). When I pray, I'm not giving You information. I'm giving You access to my heart. I'm not talking so You'll know what's happening. I'm talking so I can learn to see what You already see.

You understand things about me that I don't understand about myself. You know my internal conflicts, my mixed motives, my deepest longings. You understand why I react the way I do, why certain things trigger me, why I struggle with the same patterns.

"'For My thoughts are not your thoughts, and your ways are not My ways.' This is the Lord's declaration. 'For as heaven is higher than earth, so My ways are higher than your ways, and My thoughts than your thoughts'" (Isaiah 55:8-9).

So when I feel lost or confused, I can trust that You aren't. You see the whole picture. You know the end of the story.

If You know everything about me and still love me, then maybe I can stop hiding and rest in Your power.

You Are Omnipotent

You can do anything. I say that easily, but do I believe it?

Job believed it. "I know that You can do anything and no plan of Yours can be thwarted" (Job 42:2).

I believe, too!

Nothing is too hard for You. No situation is beyond Your reach. No heart is too broken. No life is too messed up.

When You speak, things happen. Light breaks through darkness. Dead things come to life. Storms stop. Mountains move.

"The heavens were made by the word of the Lord, and all the stars by the breath of His mouth" (Psalm 33:6).

You don't have to fight to win. You don't stress or scramble or worry about the outcome.

You just speak, and it is.

This means when I come to You with my problems, I'm not talking to a counselor or a life coach. I'm talking to the One who holds the universe together by the power of His word.

"He is before all things, and by Him all things hold together" (Colossians 1:17).

You can change anything in a moment. And if You don't, it's not because You can't. It's because You're working something deeper. Or different than what I expect or need.

Your power isn't just about miracles. It's about mercy. You could crush me for my rebellion, but instead You use Your strength to save me.

I don't have to be strong because You are strong. I get to depend on You knowing You love me.

You Are Love

You don't just love. You **are** love.

Before I was born. Before I ever prayed or believed or tried to be good. Always.

Your love isn't conditional on my behavior. It's based on Your nature. You love me because You understand exactly what I need, what my soul truly requires.

"Love consists in this: not that we loved God, but that He loved us and sent His Son to be the atoning sacrifice for our sins" (1 John 4:10).

You don't love me more when I obey and less when I fail. You don't back away when I'm struggling or withhold affection when I doubt. You understand my inconsistencies, my fears, my desperate need for acceptance.

Your love isn't fragile or fickle. It's rock-solid commitment based on Your complete understanding of who I am.

"The Lord your God is among you, a Warrior who saves. He will rejoice over you with gladness. He will be quiet in His love. He will delight in you with singing" (Zephaniah 3:17).

But Your love isn't permissive either. You love me too much to leave me stuck in patterns that destroy me. You understand my deepest longings better than I do, so You call me higher because You see what I'm truly made for.

"For the Lord disciplines the one He loves, and punishes every son He receives" (Hebrews 12:6).

You love me enough to tell me the truth. You love me enough to discipline me. You love me enough to forgive me and still call me Yours. Your love flows from Your perfect understanding of what I need most: YOU.

This love is my anchor when everything else shifts. It's my fuel when I'm running on empty. It's my hope when I can't see the way forward.

And it's the reason You hold me accountable.

You Are Just and Righteous

You are just. Always right. Never wrong.

"The Rock — His work is perfect; all His ways are just. A faithful God, without bias, He is righteous and true" (Deuteronomy 32:4).

That's hard to accept because everything around me is relative. Standards change. People compromise. But You never do. You are the definition of what's right. The measure of true justice.

"Righteousness and justice are the foundation of Your throne; faithful love and truth go before You" (Psalm 89:14).

You don't adjust Your standards based on culture or convenience. You don't play favorites or get manipulated. You see clearly and judge perfectly.

I am thankful You are not a God who lets me get away with everything. I am grateful for a God who loves me enough to tell me the truth, even when it's uncomfortable.

You don't let me take shortcuts because shortcuts don't lead to life. You hold me to Your standard because righteousness is freedom and holiness is joy.

"And He judges the world with righteousness; He executes justice on the nations with fairness" (Psalm 9:8).

When I fall short, You don't abandon me. But You don't ignore it either. You call me to repent, to return, to realign with who You created me to be.

That's love and justice working together in perfect alignment with Your mercy.

You Are Merciful

You are merciful. And I am in great need of Your mercy!

"The Lord is compassionate and gracious, slow to anger and abounding in faithful love" (Psalm 103:8).

I need Your mercy because I forget what You've said. I fail to follow through. I react out of fear instead of faith. Instead of crushing me with the justice I deserve, You meet me with mercy I don't deserve.

But this isn't pity. Your mercy flows from Your deep understanding of human frailty.

You're slow to anger because You understand my limitations. You don't pile on shame when I confess because You get how hard it is to be human. You offer help, healing, and hope because You understand exactly what I need to heal and grow.

"But You, Lord, are a compassionate and gracious, slow to anger and abounding in faithful love and truth" (Psalm 86:15).

Your mercy doesn't excuse sin. It answers it. With patience that understands my weaknesses. With correction that meets me where I am. With a path back to life that acknowledges my struggles.

You remember that I'm dust, but instead of discarding me, You draw near. You understand that I'm fragile, prone to failure, and easily overwhelmed, and You factor all of that into how You deal with me.

"As a father has compassion on his children, so the Lord shows compassion on those who fear Him. For He knows what we are made of, remembering that we are dust" (Psalm 103:13-14).

Your mercy is steady because it's based on Your understanding, not my performance. It doesn't depend on how sorry I feel or how many times I've messed up. You expected my weakness because You understand human nature completely, and You made a way through it.

You never lower Your standard, but You meet me at my failure and walk with me until I can stand again.

So I throw myself on Your mercy. Not as a way out, but as the only way forward. And I praise You for not giving me what I deserve and blessing me with more than I deserve with Your grace.

You Are Gracious

You keep giving what I could never earn.

"And God is able to make every grace overflow to you, so that in every way, always having everything you need, you may excel in every good work" (2 Corinthians 9:8).

You forgive freely. You provide faithfully. You bless abundantly.

You don't just meet the need. You go beyond it. That's how You operate.

"But He gives greater grace. Therefore He says, 'God resists the proud but gives grace to the humble'" (James 4:6).

You don't owe me anything, but You still give. Over and over. More than I ask for. More than I deserve.

You give rest when I'm striving. Peace when I'm anxious. Strength when I'm failing.

"But by the grace of God I am what I am, and His grace toward me was not in vain" (1 Corinthians 15:10a).

Your grace doesn't just clean me up. It changes me. It makes me new. It empowers me to live differently.

I didn't earn it. I can't repay it. But I can receive it and steward it well.

I don't take Your grace lightly. I don't treat it as permission to coast. I treat it as power to move forward.

Yet there is so much more to You. Show me more of who You are.

Your Personality — The Living God

You are not a force or energy or vague spiritual presence.

You are a Person. Fully alive, fully aware, fully engaged.

You have a mind that knows all things. A will that accomplishes all purposes. Emotions that respond to Your creation.

You made me in Your image. My ability to think, feel, choose, create, love all comes from You. What I express in part, You possess in full.

You are **creative**. The intricacy of the human body, the beauty of a sunset, the complexity of language — everything You make has purpose and beauty combined.

"The heavens declare the glory of God, and the expanse proclaims the work of His hands" (Psalm 19:1).

You are **joyful**. You sing over Your people. You established feasts for celebration. You rejoice when sinners repent. You designed laughter, music, play.

"You reveal the path of life to me; in Your presence is abundant joy; at Your right hand are eternal pleasures" (Psalm 16:11).

You are **patient**. Long-suffering doesn't mean passive; it means present. You stay when I drift. You endure my forgetfulness, my inconsistency, my fears.

"The Lord does not delay His promise, as some understand delay, but is patient with you, not wanting any to perish but all to come to repentance" (2 Peter 3:9).

You are **wise**. Perfect in understanding. Strategic in every action. Nothing You do is random. Nothing You allow is wasted.

"Oh, the depth of the riches both of the wisdom and knowledge of God! How unsearchable His judgments and untraceable His ways!" (Romans 11:33).

The fruit of the Spirit gives me the clearest picture of Your character: "love, joy, peace, patience, kindness, goodness, faithfulness, gentleness, and self-control" (Galatians 5:22-23).

That's who You are. When I walk with You, I begin to reflect Your character.

And You never diminish one aspect of You in favor of another. You are what I can never be: perfectly unified.

The Perfect Unity of Your Nature

You are unity without contradiction. You hold opposites I can't reconcile. Wrath and compassion. Transcendence and intimacy. In me, they war. In You, they dance.

You rule over galaxies yet know my name. You are high and lifted up, inhabiting eternity, yet You dwell with the contrite and lowly in spirit.

You are set apart in holiness yet invite me close. You uphold justice without mercy becoming cheap, and You extend mercy without justice becoming weak. In You, "faithful love and truth will join together; righteousness and peace will embrace" (Psalm 85:10).

You are the Lion and the Lamb. The Judge and the Advocate. Powerful enough to create worlds, tender enough to wipe my eyes. You speak in thunder and whisper in silence.

You know the end from the beginning, sovereign over all time, yet fully present in this moment with me.

"Remember what happened long ago, for I am God, and there is no other; I am God, and no one is like Me. I declare the end from the beginning, and from long ago what is not yet done, saying: My plan will take place, and I will do all My will" (Isaiah 46:9-10).

There's no contradiction in You. No disunity. No inconsistency.

When I feel torn between different aspects of who I am, remind me that I'm made in the image of a God who is completely whole. In You, I don't have to choose between strength and tenderness, truth and grace, justice and mercy.

You are all of it, perfectly unified.

In You, I am whole, not divided. Steady, but full of wonder. Grounded, but always growing.

Walk in Your Light

You are not a concept to study or a list of attributes to memorize.

You are the living God. Personal, powerful, holy, loving.

There's no one like You.

So I don't want to just acknowledge who You are. I want to *respond* to who You are.

I want to worship You for who You are, not just what You've done. You are always good, always right, always near, always in control. So help me trust You with my strengths and weaknesses, my failures and my fears, my successes and my future.

You've committed Yourself to me. Help me commit myself fully to You.

Help me reflect Your character in my daily life. Your righteousness, Your justice, Your mercy, Your love.

Help me faithfully walk in the light of who You are. Teach me to love others the way You love me. To rest in Your power. To listen to Your voice. To live from the truth that I am not alone.

You've made me in Your image with personality, purpose, and strength. Help me use all of it to glorify You.

I want to be like You. Not just on paper, but in practice. Not just with words, but with my life.

You are light. Help me walk in it.

In Christ,

Amen.

6

THE ACTIVE I AM

THE GOD WHO SPEAKS

FATHER,

You are the self-existent, eternal, triune, holy One who is all-powerful, all-knowing, and all-present.

And the way I know these things?

You tell me.

You speak. You communicate. You reveal Yourself.

You are not silent like the idols people create. You're not distant like the false gods we imagine. You are here. You are alive. And You have something to say.

But why do You speak? You don't need to prove anything. You don't need our applause or approval.

You speak because You care. You speak to guide, to comfort, to correct, to remind me that I'm not alone. You speak to build a relationship.

So help me tune my heart to hear You. In **Scripture**. In **creation**. In the **quiet promptings of Your Spirit**. In the **wisdom of Your people**.

That starts with contemplating the power of Your words.

The Voice That Creates

You created the universe not with Your hands, not with tools, not with existing materials.

You created everything with Your VOICE.

"Then God said, 'Let there be light,' and there was light" (Genesis 1:3).

When You spoke in the beginning of time, things that never existed suddenly appeared. Not just things. Intricately designed, perfectly balanced, stunningly beautiful things became real because You commanded them into existence.

You formed the world with WORDS out of nothing! So cool!

That makes Your voice the source of all reality.

"The heavens were made by the word of the Lord, and all the stars by the breath of His mouth" (Psalm 33:6).

Every star, every planet, every atom exists because You spoke. And You're still speaking today through what You've made, through Your Word, through Your Spirit.

If Your voice has that much power, I need to pay attention when You talk to me.

You Speak Through What You've Made

"The Mighty One God, the Lord, speaks; He summons the earth from the rising of the sun to its setting...The heavens proclaim His righteousness, for God is the Judge" (Psalm 50:1, 6).

When I step outside and really look, I hear You. Not in some vague, mystical way, but in the undeniable evidence of design.

Creation isn't silent. It shouts Your name.

The sunrise reminds me You bring light into darkness. The ocean reminds me You set boundaries that cannot be crossed. The mountains remind me You are unmovable. The flowers remind me You care about beauty, not just function.

Everything You've made points back to You. The way seasons change without fail. The way my heart beats without my permission. The way plants grow from seeds too small to see.

You are steady. Faithful. Intentional.

And you created meaning within the beauty. You put complexity into DNA and set galaxies in motion. You hold the world together with laws I can't see, and You hold my life with that same wisdom and power.

So speak to me through what You've made. Let creation remind me that You are infinite, strong, tender, and always near.

Don't let me rush past Your voice in creation. Help me slow down, listen, notice, remember.

Because everything You made shouts that You exist.

But You didn't stop speaking at creation. You keep speaking through the only book that is alive: the Bible.

You Speak Through Scripture

You didn't need a committee to create the universe. You just spoke. And with that same voice, You chose to speak through Scripture.

Over centuries. Through prophets and kings, fishermen and shepherds. Every word, every story, every line reveals Your truth.

"All Scripture is inspired by God and is profitable for teaching, for rebuking, for correcting, for training in righteousness" (2 Timothy 3:16).

Thank You for not leaving me to guess who You are. Thank You for giving me Your Word to show me.

You wrote it through people, but it came from Your Spirit. And it never loses power. It never goes out of date. It never runs dry.

As a matter of fact, it's alive.

"For the word of God is living and effective and sharper than any double-edged sword, penetrating as far as the separation of soul and spirit, joints and of marrow. It is able to judge the thoughts and intents of the heart" (Hebrews 4:12).

How is it that words written thousands of years ago can still speak directly into my life today? How can something spoken in a different culture, language, and time still breathe life into my situation?

Because it's more than words on a page. It's You speaking to me.

When I open Scripture, I experience what it's like to hear Your voice. Something clicks. Something convicts. Something comforts. And I know it's You.

You meet me in the same verses again and again, and somehow You show me something new every time.

So help me treat Your Word like the living thing it is. Not just a book to study but a conversation to have with You. Help me understand the context so I can grasp the meaning. Help me listen with my heart, not just my head.

Thank You for preserving Your Word. Thank You for speaking through human voices with divine breath.

You're not far away. You're right here, in these pages.

And You keep speaking through Your Word made flesh — Jesus.

You Speak Through Jesus

"Long ago God spoke to the fathers by the prophets at different times and in different ways. In these last days, He has spoken to us by His Son. God has appointed Him heir of all things and made the universe through Him" (Hebrews 1:1-2).

Jesus is the Word made flesh. Everything He said, everything He did, every move He made was You speaking to us.

I don't have to wonder what You're like. I can look at Jesus and know.

When He welcomed sinners, that was You. When He confronted the proud, that was You. When He healed the broken, when He wept over Jerusalem, when He died on the cross, when He rose from the tomb, that was You speaking to the world.

"The Word became flesh and dwelt among us. We observed His glory, the glory as the one and only Son from the Father, full of grace and truth" (John 1:14).

Help me not treat Jesus like a historical figure or religious symbol. Help me see Him as Your voice made visible.

He is the truth. He is the way. He is life.

Let me hear You by staying close to Him. Let me understand You by studying how He lived. Let me love You more as I follow the One who revealed You fully.

Thank You for speaking through Your Son. Through Him, I know You.

And through Your Spirit, You go even further — You come *within*.

BONNIE JEAN SCHAEFER

You Speak Through Your Spirit in Me

You didn't stop speaking with Scripture or with Jesus. You placed Your Spirit within me, and You're still speaking — quietly, clearly, faithfully — right here, right now.

"When the Spirit of truth comes, He will guide you into all the truth" (John 16:13).

Your Spirit takes what I've read in Scripture and breathes it fresh into my heart. He takes the general and makes it personal. He shows me how to apply Your truth to my specific situation.

He whispers direction into my soul. He aligns my desires with Yours. He nudges, warns, encourages, empowers.

He convicts me when I stray. He comforts me when I'm weary. He brings clarity when I'm confused.

Sometimes He just sits with me in silence and reminds me that I'm not alone.

You are here. In me. With me. For me.

"In the same way the Spirit also helps us in our weakness, because we do not know what to pray for as we should, but the Spirit Himself intercedes for us with unspoken groanings" (Romans 8:26).

So help me tune my ears to hear Your Spirit's quiet voice. Help me slow down, get still, pay attention.

And when I don't know what to say or how to pray, thank You that Your Spirit prays for me.

Thank You for speaking not just to me, but in me. When You speak in me, I'm able to speak truth to others.

And You use Your other Spirit-led children to speak to me as well.

You Speak Through Your People

You speak through Your people. Not just through pastors or teachers, but through ordinary believers who walk closely with You.

But I need discernment. I want to hear You when You speak through others, not just be swayed by good advice or impressive words.

"Dear friends, do not believe every spirit, but test the spirits to see if they are from God, because many false prophets have gone out into the world" (1 John 4:1).

Teach me to listen with wisdom. Let Your Word be my filter. Let Your Spirit be my guide. Let Your peace be my confirmation.

"But test all things. Hold on to what is good" (1 Thessalonians 5:21).

Keep me from chasing voices that sound spiritual but don't come from You. Make me quick to test what I hear against Scripture. Slow to follow hype. Steady in truth.

Show me the difference between someone who talks about You and someone You're actually speaking through.

And I don't just want to hear from others. I want You to speak through me. Make me trustworthy. Humble. Grounded in Your Word. Sensitive to Your Spirit.

Let my words build up, not tear down. Let me speak when You say speak and stay quiet when You haven't given me anything to say.

I don't want to be impressive. I want to be *useful*.

Shape my heart so Your voice can flow through it in a way that doesn't add noise but adds depth. Because this world is loud.

Recognizing Your Voice in a Noisy World

Information is everywhere. Books, podcasts, social media, videos, courses, opinions. With a few clicks, I can get instant advice, endless answers, and trending truth.

But access comes with a cost: distraction, confusion, even deception. The more voices I listen to, the harder it becomes to recognize the One voice that matters most: Yours.

I can get answers in seconds, but what I need is Your answer. Not the fastest or the loudest. Yours.

"My sheep hear My voice, I know them, and they follow Me" (John 10:27).

I am Your sheep. Because I belong to You, I can hear You. But I must tune my heart to listen.

Help me turn down the volume of the world so I can turn toward You.

I don't want to be swept away by what's trending. I don't want to chase what's easy or popular. I want what's true. I want what's You. Teach me to pause before I follow any voice. To test every word I take in. To hold up every "truth" to the light of Your truth.

Give me ears trained by Scripture. A heart that listens for Your Spirit's tone. A mind that recognizes the difference between hype and holiness.

And don't just help me hear You. Help me follow You. Because sometimes I hear, but I still hesitate. I still chase faster answers.

So pull me back. Call me out. Remind me: Your voice is enough.

But what do I do when I can't hear You?

When You Seem Silent

Sometimes I hear You clearly through Your Word and in the stillness through Your Spirit.

But there are times when I strain to hear You and am greeted with silence. I seek an answer, and none comes.

In those moments, it feels like You're far away.

Yet I know You haven't moved. You don't change. You don't sleep. You don't forget about me.

"God is not man, that He might lie, or a son of man, that He might change His mind. Does He speak and not act, or promise and not fulfill?" (Numbers 23:19).

When I cry out and get no answer, help me believe You're still near. When I open my Bible and it feels dry, help me remember Your Word is still alive. When my world turns upside down, ground me in what's true.

You are the God who speaks. Even when I can't hear You.

Give me faith that doesn't fold in the silence. Give me discipline that keeps seeking when emotions fade. Give me patience that endures through the waiting.

And if You're quiet because You want to deepen my hunger for You, then deepen it. Strip away every substitute. Make me still. Make me desperate. Make me faithful.

Because when I cannot hear You, it's not because You are silent. It's because I must trust what You have already said.

Tuned to Your Voice

You are the God who speaks.

You spoke the universe into existence, and You're still speaking now. Through Scripture, creation, Jesus, Your Spirit, Your people.

You speak in loud moments and quiet ones. In clarity and mystery. In storms and stillness.

Your voice isn't always loud, but it's always true. It's not always immediate, but it's always faithful.

Tune my heart to hear You. Train my ears to know Your tone. Keep me close enough that even Your whispers change me.

When the world gets loud or You seem quiet, let me stay rooted in truth.

I surrender my ears, my heart, my mind. Teach me to recognize Your voice. Teach me to trust what You have spoken. Teach me to obey, even when I don't understand.

So speak, Lord, for Your servant is listening.

In Christ,

Amen.

7

THE TRANSFORMING I AM

LIVING IN LIGHT OF WHO GOD IS

FATHER,

You reveal Yourself as the Great I AM — self-existent, eternal, unchanging. You show me Your holiness, wisdom, power, and love wrapped in Your triune nature. You speak to me and with me and in me and through me.

You fellowship with me, renew my mind, and transform me from the inside out.

To know You is what I was created for. To walk with You. To be changed by You. To reflect You.

Knowing You is the beginning of transformation. And as a sinner, I am in desperate need of transformation.

This isn't just intellectual knowledge. Knowing You is a life-changing encounter with the living God.

The Impact of Knowing You

My great desire is to be transformed into Your image so that I become like Christ in all I think, all I say, and all I do.

That starts with renewing my mind in light of who You are.

Knowing You as the Great I AM means You are self-existent. Independent. Unchanging. You need nothing. You depend on no one.

I am not like You. You are the source of my life, my strength, my identity. I need You to survive while You need no one.

So why do I try to live like I'm self-sufficient? What a futile mission that leads to emptiness and striving!

Because You are the Great I AM, I get to stop being independent. I get to stop performing, proving, working to achieve all these dreams You've planted in me on my own strength.

I get to surrender. To draw everything I need from You. I get to live in complete dependence on Your power.

Knowing You as the Eternal One means You are outside of time. Sovereign over it. Never rushed. Never delayed.

So why do I panic about my plans?

Knowing You are Eternal means I live differently. I get to trust Your timing. I get to prepare for eternity. I get to make decisions in light of forever, not just today.

Because although my soul has a beginning, it has no end. This life will end because sin brought death into the world, but Christ settled my sin debt so I can come boldly into Your presence when this life is through.

Heaven isn't a maybe. It's a certainty. And I live now to get ready for what's next.

Knowing You as the Triune God means You are three-in-one: Father, Son, Spirit. A community of perfect unity and love.

I can't fully comprehend that design, but I believe it.

It shapes how I live. I pursue peace with You, within myself, and with others.

And it informs how I pray. Because You are triune, I pray to the Father, through the Son, by the power of the Spirit.

Knowing You as the Holy One means You are pure. Set apart. And You call me to be holy like You.

That doesn't mean I'm perfect, but it does mean different.

I resist sin. I fight compromise. I confess quickly. I choose purity over popularity.

You've given me Your Spirit. You've broken the power of sin in my life, enabling me to walk the path of righteousness even though it's not popular or easy.

But it's worth every step.

Knowing You as the God with perfect character means You're always here, always faithful, limitless in love, grace, mercy, justice, and creativity.

I get to trust You fully, even when I don't understand. I get to rest in Your promises knowing they cannot fail. I get to walk in peace because You are unchanging.

And knowing You as the God who speaks means I get to have a relationship with You.

You speak through Your Word, through creation, through Christ, through Your Spirit, through Your people. You never leave me guessing.

So I tune in. I pay attention. I listen. I don't chase the loudest voice. I follow Your voice.

You are everything I'm not AND everything I need. So take all of me. Make me holy, humble, bold, compassionate, and relentless like You.

The Transformation of Life

If I truly know You — if I truly see You for who You are — then I can't stay the same.

You are the Only I AM. And when I follow You, everything in me must change.

Change how I see myself. I want to remember that I am God-created, not self-made. That makes me fully dependent on You, not independent of Your authority. And that means I'm set apart for Your glory rather than condemned to live an invisible or ordinary life.

Because of You, my identity is no longer built on performance, approval, or comparison. It's anchored in You and who You say I am.

"But you are a chosen race, a royal priesthood, a holy nation, a people for His possession, that you may proclaim the praises of the One who called you out of darkness into His marvelous light" (1 Peter 2:9).

Change how I live. Show me how to glorify You, not feed my selfish desires. Plant desires in my heart that lead to eternal impact, not temporary success. Keep me focused on knowing You as my top priority so I don't get swept up chasing the empty pleasures of this world.

"Do not be conformed to this age, but be transformed by the renewing of your mind, so that you may discern what is the good, pleasing, and perfect will of God" (Romans 12:2).

Give me vision that lasts longer than this life.

Change how I love. Teach me to reflect the love You show, love that is sacrificial, selfless, committed. Help me build real relationships filled with peace, joy, and purpose.

"By this everyone will know that you are My disciples, if you love one another" (John 13:35).

Guard my heart. Shape my boundaries. Let the way I connect with others reflect Your truth and grace.

And change who I'm becoming. Grow me in holiness. Let my thoughts and actions mirror You. Let the fruit of Your Spirit overflow in me so my life is marked by love, mercy, justice, and truth.

I don't want to conform to this world. I long to be transformed by Your Word.

You've revealed Yourself so I could reflect You. Not just for a moment, but for eternity. And I get to practice for eternity in the day to day life of the here and now.

The Practice of Knowing You

Head knowledge of You is useless if it doesn't flow into my heart and through my daily actions.

If I claim to know You, then my life should bear witness to that truth.

I pray like I'm standing before the Holy One. I speak to my King and Creator, my Father and Friend.

I pray with reverence and boldness. With trust and honesty.

I pray like I know who You are and who I am in You. Like I believe You're listening and have the power to move mountains.

"Therefore, let us approach the throne of grace with boldness, so that we may receive mercy and find grace to help us in time of need" (Hebrews 4:16).

I pray for impossible things because nothing is impossible with You.

I worship with wonder that flows from all I know about You. I worship with my words, my songs, my work, my very life.

"Therefore, brothers and sisters, in view of the mercies of God, I urge you to present your bodies as a living sacrifice, holy and pleasing to God; this is your true worship" (Romans 12:1).

I serve because I've been rescued. Because Your Spirit fills me. Because You deserve everything I've got.

I serve with excellence and joy, even if no one sees, even if it costs me everything because You gave everything for me.

I witness with my life as well as my words. Because a life of holiness is powerless if people around me don't know why I choose to live differently.

Make me bold. Make me bright. Let my life shout: Jesus is Lord.

"In the same way, let your light shine before others, so that they may see your good works and give glory to your Father in heaven" (Matthew 5:16).

I work with integrity. I create with intention. I solve real problems. I serve real people.

I work to bring dreams to life, dreams that are worth pursuing because they come from You and arise from my delight in knowing You.

And I rest with joy. After all, You command celebration. You built feasts into the law.

Let me laugh without guilt and rest on purpose.

Through it all — praying, worshiping, serving, witnessing, working, resting — never let me settle for today's level of knowledge when there's always more to learn.

The Lifelong Adventure

To know You is not something I check off a list. It's a lifelong pursuit. An eternal adventure.

I don't want to settle for what I already know. I want to go deeper. Clearer vision. Stronger faith. Sharper discernment.

The more I walk with You, the more I want to walk even closer. Because there is always more of You to know.

"This what the Lord says: 'The wise person should not boast in his wisdom; the strong should not boast in his strength; the wealthy should not boast in his wealth. But the one who boasts should boast in this: that he understands and knows Me — that

I am the Lord, showing faithful love, justice, and righteousness on the earth, for I delight in these things.' This is the Lord's declaration" (Jeremiah 9:23-24).

Let that truth fuel my hunger. Let it crush my pride. Remind me that I have not arrived or figured You out.

I need You to change the way I think. Interrupt my assumptions. Rewire my thoughts. Renew my mind with Your Word so I walk in step with You.

I want to experience You daily. To hear You, follow You, obey You, reflect You.

I will never reach the end of You. Not in this life. Not in the next. Because You are infinite.

So I will spend forever going deeper, climbing higher, leaning in closer.

Let this be my lifelong cry: God, I want to know You more. Whatever it costs. However long it takes.

I want to know You more.

And when I hit the limit of what I can understand, expand my heart and mind and soul and remind me that You know me completely.

The Wonder of Being Known

You know me. All the way through. Every hidden thought. Every unchecked motive. Every contradiction. Every doubt. Every fear.

You know the parts of me I hide from everyone else. And You love me anyway.

You understand me. You get why I react the way I do. You understand the wounds that make me defensive, the insecurities that drive my people-pleasing, the fears that keep me awake at night.

You understand my past and how it shaped me. You see the scars I carry and understand exactly how they affect my present struggles.

You understand my personality and the way I process emotions, the way I need encouragement, the way I show love. You understand my unique gifts and calling, even when I don't fully grasp them myself.

You understand my future fears, the "what ifs" that paralyze me, the dreams I'm afraid to pursue, the ways I worry about failing or succeeding.

Nothing about me surprises You. You're not waiting for me to get my life together before I'm worthy of Your presence. You're not thrown off by my questions or my weakness. You understand my internal contradictions — how I can love You and struggle with doubt, how I can want to obey and still wrestle with sin.

You already knew what You were getting when You saved me, and You saved me anyway.

I can't disappoint You into leaving. I can't fail enough to lose Your love. You don't walk away when I fall. Instead, You reach for me. Every time.

Because You don't just love me emotionally. You love me eternally. You don't just know my actions. You understand my heart. You don't just forgive me once. You keep transforming me. Slowly. Deeply. Patiently.

You understand me better than I understand myself. When I feel lost in my own confusion, You see clearly. When I'm overwhelmed by my contradictions, You hold all the pieces together with perfect understanding.

This is the wonder: The all-knowing, all-holy, all-powerful God who understands every nuance of who I am...wants me. Wants to be known by me. Wants to walk with me. Wants to shape me.

You see through all my pretending to what I really need. You understand my heart when I can't find words. You get what I'm going through when everyone else misses it completely.

The Eternal Perspective

This journey of knowing You doesn't end when this life does. It's just beginning.

"For now we see only a reflection, but then face to face. Now I know in part, but then I will know fully, as I am fully known" (1 Corinthians 13:12).

One day I will see You face to face. The mystery will become clear. The questions will be answered. The longing will be fulfilled.

But even then, even in Your presence, I will spend eternity discovering new depths of who You are. Because You are infinite, and I am finite.

Heaven won't be boring. It will be the ultimate adventure of knowing You without the barriers of sin, without the limitations of this broken world.

Until that day, I live with hope. I walk by faith. I press on toward the goal.

"My goal is to know Him and the power of His resurrection and the fellowship of His sufferings, being conformed to His death, assuming that I will somehow reach the resurrection from among the dead" (Philippians 3:10-11).

So here I am. Fully seen. Fully known. Fully loved.

And I'll spend the rest of my life — and all of eternity — learning what that really means.

You are THE ONLY I AM. And I am Yours. Forever.

In Christ,

Amen

ACKNOWLEDGEMENTS

To my parents — Harry and Janice Schaefer: Thank you for raising me in the fear and knowledge of the Lord, for modeling what it means to walk with God daily, and for reviewing this manuscript to ensure theological accuracy. Mom, thank you for leading me to Christ. Father, that you for faithfully teaching the word and shaping my understanding of who God is.

To my pastor — John Holmes: Thank you for taking the time to review this manuscript and provide feedback. Your commitment to sound doctrine and your pastoral heart have been invaluable in ensuring this book points people to Christ.

To every reader: Thank you for choosing to anchor your faith in the unchanging God. My prayer is that this book deepens your relationship with the Only I AM.

ABOUT THE AUTHOR

BONNIE JEAN SCHAEFER IS the Adventurous Author who adventurizes life.

She's on a mission to anchor Christians in who God is so they know who they are — and then live boldly from that place. Her framework? **Start with WHO. And WHO starts with God.**

A lifelong Christian with a Bible degree from Cedarville College (now Cedarville University), Bonnie hosts *The Adventurous Author* podcast and founded Dream Doers Publishing. She writes under her own name for faith and writing content and as D.K. Drake for the *Dragon Stalker Bloodlines* fantasy saga.

The same woman who's crossed five marathon finish lines and tackled 50K trail races approaches faith with equal intensity. She lives in North Carolina with her two sisters, raising four adopted children and proving that anchored people live adventurously as Dream Doers.

The 50 by 50 Mission

Bonnie is publishing 50 books by her 50th birthday. The mission started on her 48th birthday to challenge her to finish books in various stages of the writing process: *The Faithful Christian Living Experience* (12 foundational books), *The Wealthy Writer Experience* (training for God's creatives), and 35+ children's stories through the *Everrlyn Experience* and *Zella Zeal Experience*.

This is book 1 of 50.

Join the adventure at TheAdventurousAuthor.com/league for monthly storytelling tournaments, weekly sparks, and the digital version of every book as it releases — just $7/month.

What adventure is God prompting YOU to start?

— • —

WHY THIS SERIES EXISTS

THE FAITHFUL CHRISTIAN LIVING EXPERIENCE

DEAR READER,

I am not writing these books because I have all the answers. I'm writing them because I have all the questions.

I wanted answers to my questions, so I studied Bible in college and kept digging long after I earned that degree. I gained solid theological knowledge. But knowledge alone wasn't enough.

I could live it with quiet conviction, but I couldn't synthesize it. I couldn't articulate it with clarity. And I didn't have the boldness to speak up and speak out in a way God was calling me to.

So a few years ago, I wanted to distill everything I'd learned from Scripture into a framework that felt like a story rather than systematic theology — a framework I could actually live and speak from, not just study. I wanted to connect the dots in a way that anchored my soul, fueled my faith, and helped me related to my God effectively.

So I started pray-thinking in my journal, wrestling with the foundational questions every Christian needs to answer:

- **Who is God?** What is He like? What makes Him unique?

- **Who is God in relation to me?** Is He distant? Engaged? What does it mean that He calls Himself Creator, King, Judge, Savior, Father, Friend, and Helper?

- **What does God want, and why?** What are His driving purposes, and how does He accomplish them?

- **Why should I trust the Bible?** What makes it different from every other religious text? In a world of noise and deception, how do I know what's real?

- **What happens after I die?** Is eternity real or just a comforting story?

- **Who is Satan?** What does my greatest enemy want, and how does he try to get it?

- **Why do I matter?** What's my purpose in God's eternal plan?

- **How did God design me?** What does it mean to be made in His image — heart, mind, body, and soul?

- **How do I live from this foundation?** What values guide me? What's my character foundation? How do I set goals that honor God?

The Faithful Christian Living Experience books are the result of that wrestling. They are designed to give you a framework for knowing God, understanding yourself, and living faithfully in a world that's hostile to truth.

These 11 catalyst books are designed to anchor your faith:

- **Anchored Faith** (Books 1-3) — Know God, Trust God, Walk with God

- **Anchored Truth** (Books 4-6) — Explore why the Bible is true, the reality of eternity, and your invisible enemy (and how to fight him effectively)

- **Anchored Identity** (Books 7-8) — Discover who you are in Christ and why you are significant

- **Anchored Living** (Books 9-11) — Walk out what you've learned in a way that aligns with God and your design

These aren't theology textbooks. They're conversations with God about identity: His, mine, and yours. Each book builds on the foundation laid before it, because you can't discern truth without first knowing God. You know who you are without building on TRUTH. You can't live effectively without knowing who you are IN CHRIST.

This is the hard work of building unshakeable faith that withstands storms, resists deception, and finishes what God starts.

You'll never reach the end of knowing God. He's infinite, and you're finite. But that's makes seeking Him a thrilling adventure — one that carries through from this life into eternity.

And you don't have to walk this journey alone.

In Christ,

Bonnie Jean Schaefer

P.S. I'd love to hear how this book has impacted your relationship with God. Please share your story as an email to me (bonnie@adventurizelife.com) or as a review on Amazon.

Join the Adventure at TheAdventuruousAuthor.com.

— • —

THE LEAGUE OF ADVENTUROUS AUTHORS

FOR YEARS, I CALLED myself an "aspiring writer." I had the calling. I had the faith. I had stories burning in my bones.

But I couldn't finish anything.

Random writing bursts. Broken promises. Guilt every time I chose writing over family time. The loop of starting projects and abandoning them at Chapter 3.

That's why I built **The League of Adventurous Authors™**—because I needed the flexible lifestyle system rooted in Christ I couldn't find anywhere else.

It's a Christ-anchored training league that fixes **Creative Identity first** (just like this book anchored you in who God is and who you are in Him), then builds the rhythm that actually lasts.

If you're a Christian fiction author ready to:
– Stop calling yourself "aspiring"
– Write consistently without guilt
– Finish stories you start
– Train for faithfulness, not fame
– ENJOY the process of doing hard things...

Join me in The League at TheAdventurousAuthor.com/league or listen to The Adventurous Author podcast.

Let's train together.

www.ingramcontent.com/pod-product-compliance
Lightning Source LLC
Chambersburg PA
CBHW031632040426
42452CB00007B/796